Science on the Edge

CHASING TORNADOES

LAURIE LINDOP

Twenty-First Century Books / Brookfield, Connecticut

Dedicated to Erik Abdow

Front cover photograph courtesy of © Howard B. Bluestein
Back cover photograph courtesy of Photo Researchers, Inc © Howard B. Bluestein

Photographs courtesy of National Oceanic & Atmospheric Administration (NOAA): pp. 4 (Dr. Joseph Golden); NOAA Photo Library, NOAA Central Library; OAR/ERL/National Severe Storms Laboratory (NSSL): pp. 17, 25, 37, 38, 40, 41, 42, 45, 46, 48, 59; FEMA News Photo: p. 11 (Dave Saville); Ron Miller: p. 18; Photo Researchers, Inc.: pp. 15 (© Howard B. Bluestein), 19 (© E. R. Degginger), 20-21 (© Howard B. Bluestein), 24 (© David R. Frazier), 27 (© Howard B. Bluestein), 34 (© Howard B. Bluestein); © Howard B. Bluestein: pp. 32, 63, 70; National Center for Atmospheric Research/University Corporation for Atmospheric Research/National Science Foundation: pp. 29, 31 (both); © David O. Blanchard, NOAA/National Severe Storms Laboratory: p. 30; Kansas State Historical Society: p. 50; Tinker Air Force Base History Office: p. 54; University of Chicago: p. 57; Dr. Bruce D. Lee, University of Northern Colorado and Robert B. Wilhelmson, University of Illinois: p. 65; Wind Science and Engineering Research Center, Texas Tech University, Lubbock, Texas: pp. 67, 68

Library of Congress Cataloging-in-Publication Data
Lindop, Laurie.
Chasing tornadoes / by Laurie Lindop.
v. cm.—(Science on the edge)
Includes bibliographical references and index.
Contents: Tornado!—Tornado research—Project Vortex—
History of tornado science—When a tornado strikes.
ISBN 0-7613-2703-7 (lib. bdg.)
1. Tornadoes—Juvenile literature.   2. Meteorologists—
Juvenile literature. [1. Tornadoes. 2. Meteorologists.]
I. Title.   II. Series.
QC955.2   .L56   2003
551.55'3—dc21   2002014250

Published by Twenty-First Century Books
A Division of The Millbrook Press, Inc.
2 Old New Milford Road
Brookfield, Connecticut 06804
www.millbrookpress.com

CONTENTS

This photo of a waterspout was taken by tornado scientist Joe Golden, who flew through a similar one during a research mission.

Introduction

In Key West, Florida, a young tornado researcher named Joe Golden climbed aboard a small, sturdy airplane that was loaded with weather sensors. "Golden, you idiot," he thought to himself, "are you sure you should be doing this?"[1]

The plane rumbled down the runway and lifted off. The pilot flew over Florida's blue-green water and Golden peered out his window looking for a waterspout. Waterspouts are tornadoes that form over water instead of land. They make good research subjects for tornado scientists because they are usually less powerful than land tornadoes, although some are strong enough to suck up fish, seaweed, and even boats. If they come ashore, they can wreck docks and blow apart buildings.

After awhile, Golden spotted a waterspout off in the distance. It looked like a gray thread dangling from the base of a storm cloud. As the plane roared closer, the waterspout became a shimmery funnel like the tornado in *The Wizard of Oz*. Golden gripped his armrests with "white knuckles and gritted [his] teeth, holding on for dear life."[2] They were about to do something that no one had ever dared try—fly straight through a twisting waterspout. Golden knew there was a significant possibility that the plane might spin out of control as soon as it hit the swirling waterspout, but he was driven by a scientist's insatiable curiosity to find out what happens inside its funnel.

He hoped for the best as the pilot aimed the plane's nose straight for the waterspout. Up close, it looked like a shear, rippling veil. As they hit the veil, the plane lurched violently. Golden felt his teeth rattle and he was pushed out of his seat and then thrown straight back into it. In less than a second, they'd passed through and emerged safely out the other side. The plane's special weather sensors had gathered valuable data about the wind speed and pressure drop inside the funnel.

Golden's work is part of the exciting field of tornado science. These daredevil scientists are known as "storm chasers" because they leave their labs in order to chase after the storms that cause tornadoes. Sometimes they conduct their experiments from airplanes, but mostly they use specially equipped cars and trucks to pursue land-based tornadoes. If they find a tornado, they try to probe it with a variety of sensing devices. As they conduct their experiments, they can expect to encounter hail, gale-force winds, and dangerous lightning. The highly trained tornado hunters can easily end up as the hunted when a twister suddenly switches direction and comes straight at them.

Tornado scientists go out on the edge to gather data about the deadliest storms on Earth because they hope that their research will eventually lead to more accurate tornado forecasts and save people's lives. "We think we know what we're doing," said leading researcher Howard Bluestein. "Lion tamers work with lions and probably aren't worried about getting their heads bitten off. We may feel the same way [about tornadoes]."[3]

CHAPTER ONE

Tornado!

April 21, 2001, was prom night in Hoisington, Kansas. As kids drove up to the Knights of Columbus Hall, a drizzly rain was falling. After about an hour of dancing, the lights started to flicker on and off. A few minutes later the whole auditorium went dark and the music died. A strong wind sucked the doors open, and the kids could see rain lashing down horizontally. To keep everyone entertained, the DJ found a stick to use as a limbo bar and couples started lining up to duck under it hoping that soon the power would come back on. The high school principal stepped outside to survey the storm just as an ambulance raced down the block. An announcement to take cover blared over the ambulance's public address system. The principal ran back into the hall and shouted for everyone to go down into the basement.

The kids wanted to know what was going on—maybe a severe thunderstorm or even a tornado? "At this point it would only be speculation," the principal told them.[1]

Across town at the Dairy Queen, Gloria Adams recalled hearing a frightening roar at about 9:30 at night. "People are describing it as a freight train. I don't know if it sounded like a freight train, it was the most horrible roar I've ever heard in my life."[2]

Realizing it was a tornado, the restaurant owner shouted for everyone to hide in the walk-in cooler. Before Adams could get there, the Dairy Queen's roof was yanked away. Debris flew through the restaurant. Napkins whirled like white confetti, boards slammed into the counter, dishes and silverware flew out into the dark chaotic night. Adams fell to her hands and knees to try to avoid getting hit. The ferocious wind felt like a hand holding her back as she crawled around the corner to huddle with five other employees inside the cooler. "It's not very big," Adams remembered, "this cooler where they keep, oh, like their Dairy Queen toppings for their ice cream and stuff like that."[3]

Clinging to each other in terror, they heard the tornado rip the building apart. "Everyone was just so scared," Adams recalled. "We cried; we yelled; we prayed. . . . God please let us get out of this alive."[4] And then it was all over. The roaring monster was gone. Gloria Adams and the other employees pushed open the cooler door and stared at the rubble. It looked like a bomb had gone off.

Across town the kids at the prom were still in the basement, unaware of what had happened outside. Some used their cell phones to call friends and family. One girl recalled that rumors were flying: "All of a sudden someone pops up and says, 'Zack, your house is gone.' . . . And then it was all of Fifth Street's gone and all of Sixth Street's gone. . . . There are people crying because we can't leave and we don't know where our families are. . . . All I could do was cry."[5]

When they finally went upstairs, the air was cool and the power was out on Main Street, but otherwise everything looked fine. Police cars, ambulances, and fire trucks sped by, brightening up the night with their flashing red-and-blue lights. Parents started arriving and the kids could tell by their expressions that something awful had happened. One boy said, "I walked up to [my mom] and she started crying and my sister was sitting there crying and I was just like oh no. . . . I kind of sat there and I didn't believe it at first. . . . A tornado . . . How could there be a tornado without us knowing?"[6]

One girl ran home in her prom dress leaping over fallen tree limbs and downed power lines. When she got there, she found the roof had been ripped off her house. More than four hundred homes were either damaged or totally lost, but only one person, an elderly man, died—a remarkable statistic considering that the tornado cut from one end of town to the other, creating a six-block, mile-long path of destruction.

Every year eight hundred tornadoes strike the United States and, on average, 80 people die and 1,500 people are injured. It is

These houses were in the path of destruction when a tornado swept through Hoisington, Kansas, in April 2001.

very difficult to predict exactly where and when a tornado will strike. At best, forecasters can say that in the next eight to twelve hours there *might* be some thunderstorms that *might* produce one or more tornadoes over a large area that may include a number of different states. An hour or so in advance, scientists can narrow down the region likely to be hit, but they can't say for certain whether or not a tornado will form, how big it will be, and what path it will take. Once the storm starts to show telltale rotation or a funnel appears, they can issue tornado warnings that give people, on average, between eleven minutes and half an hour to seek shelter.

That's not much time, but as recently as 1986, the National Weather Service was providing only four and a half minutes of lead time on its average tornado warnings. The improvement was due in large part to research done by a group of tornado scientists who are hard at work right now in a part of the United States known as Tornado Alley.

Birth of a Twister

Tornado Alley is a region that roughly encompasses the states lying between the Mississippi River and the high plains—mainly Texas, Oklahoma, Kansas, Nebraska, Iowa, Missouri, Arkansas, and Louisiana. Each spring the weather conditions there are perfect for producing the powerful thunderstorms that cause tornado outbreaks. Scientists flock to this area because while tornadoes occur in many parts of the world and have struck in every state of the union, nowhere on Earth are they as common as in Tornado Alley.

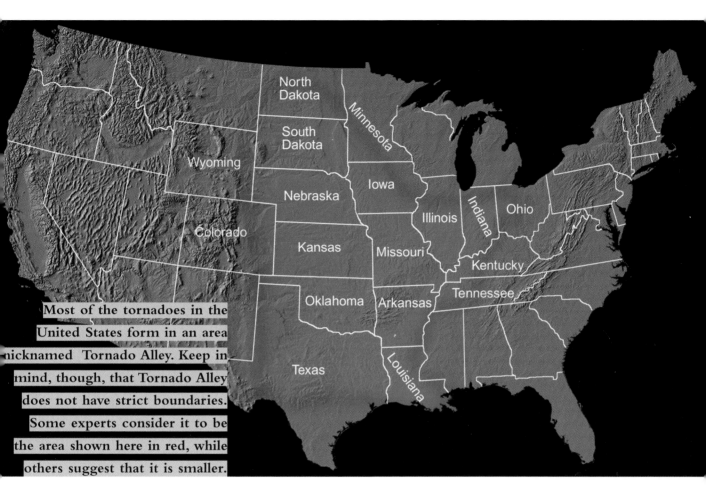

Most of the tornadoes in the United States form in an area nicknamed Tornado Alley. Keep in mind, though, that Tornado Alley does not have strict boundaries. Some experts consider it to be the area shown here in red, while others suggest that it is smaller.

Here, from April through June, very warm moist air from the Gulf of Mexico rushes northward where it encounters winds blowing in from central Mexico to the southwest. At an even higher altitude, cold winds gust in from the Rockies. *Wind shear* is the word meteorologists use to describe winds that blow in different directions at different altitudes.

Generally, warm air wants to rise. As it does, it encounters the wind shear and starts to rotate. To understand why, imagine making a snake out of clay: You put a ball of clay on one palm and then roll it back and forth between both palms. As you do so, one hand goes away from you while the other hand comes back toward you, and the clay rotates into a snake. Similarly, air will spin in an invisible horizontal tube (a snake shape) when one wind above pushes it going one way and another wind below pushes it going the other.

While the air is rotating like this, the sun is also heating the ground, which causes upward-moving currents. The currents eventually jerk the rotating air into a vertical position (so that the snake is standing on its tail).

Now this tube of intensely rotating air acts like a vacuum hose feeding hot, moist air from the ground up into the higher levels of the atmosphere. As this air rises, it cools and turns into condensation (water droplets). The water droplets make thunder-clouds. As more warm air continues to get sucked up, the thunderclouds bubble upward looking like shaving cream mountains in the sky.

Eventually the clouds will reach an altitude where they can no longer keep rising, usually between 30,000 and 50,000 feet (9,144 and 15,240 meters). At these heights, the cloud tops become filled with ice crystals and snowflakes. These powerful thunderstorms with deeply rotating and long-lived updrafts are called *supercells.* Supercells will often send hail and lightning slashing to the ground. One tornado researcher recalled driving through such a fearsome hailstorm that both the front and back windshields shattered. "We kept driving anyway," he said. "Little slivers of glass were everywhere. My driver got slivers in his face;

Supercell thunderstorms can produce severe weather.

I got them in my laptop computer while I was typing on it. . . . I put my clipboard against the windshield for some protection."[7]

In a supercell there is an area of strong rotation called the *mesocyclone.* Some mesocyclones (though not all) give birth to tornadoes. If a tornado is going to form, several events tend to occur almost simultaneously: The mesocyclone tightens its rotation. The tighter it gets, the faster it spins, in the same way that figure skaters will spin faster when they draw their arms in close to their bodies. Rotating violently, the mesocyclone then moves to the rear of the storm. From the ground, you might see a rotating section of cloud drop from the storm's southwestern base, looking like a boat's rudder. This rudder-shaped cloud is called the rotating *wall cloud.* Tornado researchers know that the appearance of a wall cloud means that it is show time and tornadoes may start twisting at any minute.

While all of this is going on, a clearly defined cascade of warm humid air also flows downward from the storm's rear. This is called the Rear Flank Downdraft (RFD). The RFD is strong enough to shake cars, knock down power lines, and send farm equipment tumbling. Tornado researchers call this violent rear area of the storm "the bear's cage" because to get under it can be as deadly as walking into a grizzly bear's cage.

Greg Forbes, a severe-weather expert, explained that while scientists don't know all the forces that cause the rotation in the mesocyclone to reach the ground, in general, "thunderstorm downdrafts or other processes allow some of the rotation aloft to reach or develop at the surface. At that point, updrafts can concentrate this low-level rotation into a . . . tornado."[8]

In movies and on television tornadoes are almost always depicted as whirling funnel clouds, but tornadoes and funnel clouds are actually a little bit different. A tornado is simply defined as a violently rotating column of air in contact with the ground and related to a thunderstorm. Inside tornadoes, funnel

A wall cloud, shown here, occurs when a cloud base lowers from underneath a main storm. Wall clouds usually develop from a few minutes up to an hour before a tornado forms.

This diagram shows the components of a tornadic thunderstorm.

MESOCYCLONE

REAR FLANK
DOWNDRAFT

TORNADO

WALL CLOUD

clouds form when the air flowing into them contains water vapor. It is this vapor that whirls from the clouds in a funnel shape. Other tornadoes form without funnels and are invisible except for the damage they cause as they whip up dust, vegetation, trash, and more.

Not all tornadoes create funnels like the one shown here. Some tornadoes are invisible.

Studying the Skies

Tornado scientists are expert cloud-gazers. They look for various clues in a thunderstorm to figure out whether a tornado is likely to appear. Newspaper reporter Joe Nick Patoski joined a group of expert storm chasers and was impressed by the things they saw in a storm that he, as a layperson, didn't understand:

> An ominous black cloud hovered overhead, throwing off bolts of lightning that sparked grass fires which sent billows of smoke hundreds of feet high. ... Close by I spotted black swirls rising above one of the fires. "Tornado!" I thought and held my breath. But no, I was told, it was ... created by a downdraft from within the storm. ... Amid the fire and rain, the chasers kept their eyes on a wispy dark cloud that emerged from the base of the storm. They were waiting for it to rotate ... As I nervously surveyed the roiling mass, I was again certain a tornado would soon drop. But the storm chasers saw things in the explosive weather that I could not. The edges of the cloud base were not sharply defined, indicating that the storm was weakening. ... There wasn't the right mix of warm and cold air needed to make a tornado. As the grass fires glowed in the dusk beneath a flashing angry sky, we chased clouds south and west for another hundred miles [161 km] before calling it a day.[9]

A potentially tornadic thunderstorm forms rotating clouds in Oklahoma.

21

CHAPTER TWO

Chasing Twisters out on the Plains

A number of our nation's top tornado researchers work out of the National Severe Storms Laboratory (NSSL) and the University of Oklahoma, both of which are located in Norman, Oklahoma, right in the heart of Tornado Alley. During tornado season, these scientists put everything else in their lives on hold and dedicate themselves to storm chasing. It's a race against the clock to gather data from as many tornadoes as possible. A lot of the time their storm chase ends in disappointment—only about one out of every ten supercell storms will actually produce a tornado.

22

"People who drive thousands of miles in pursuit of tornadoes might see at most a few a year," said Howard Bluestein. "People who do not chase them probably will never see any at all. That is why we tornado scientists sometimes envy our colleagues who concern themselves with fixed objects of study such as rocks, microscope slides, or the moon. Our subjects are more like living creatures—enormous . . . animals that appear fleetingly and unpredictably at places they choose."[1]

The Art of the Forecast

Scientists don't head out blindly and hope they'll find a tornado. Before hitting the road, they study computerized weather maps looking for places where severe weather is likely to form later in the day. These forecasts rely on weather satellites orbiting the planet and special Doppler radar towers positioned across Tornado Alley. Each radar tower has a rotating dishlike antenna that shoots a radio wave out into the atmosphere. If the beam hits any precipitation (rain, hail, snow, etc.), part of that energy scatters back to the radar's antenna. These returned signals reveal not only the intensity of the precipitation but also the motion in and around the storm. In fact, the Tornado Alley Doppler radar network is so powerful it can detect bats and clouds of insects flying 60 miles (97 kilometers) away![2]

Ideally, researchers want to arrive at an area just as a supercell thunderstorm starts to develop. That way, if a tornado forms, they can gather data from the moment of its birth until it dissipates. On days when it looks like severe weather could occur in a number of different regions, researchers make an educated guess as to which storm to pursue. "Often it comes down to

In a Doppler radar tower, the rotating dish that sends out radio waves is located in the globe at the top.

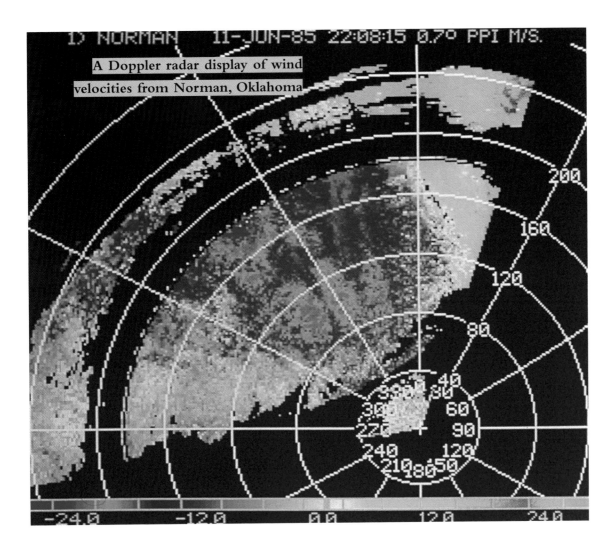

A Doppler radar display of wind velocities from Norman, Oklahoma

choosing between one storm or another storm and half the time you're right and half the time you're wrong," said Howard Bluestein.[3]

The shortness of the tornado season combined with the hit-and-miss aspect to chasing can make it stressful. Robert Davies-Jones, a seasoned veteran, said, "You go out [to the countryside], and you get anxious: Are there going to be storms? Are you going to be in the right spot? You start second guessing. . . . Anxiety mounts."[4] His colleague Tim Marshall agreed: "There is nothing more frustrating than to drive hundreds of miles only to sit around in some remote place on the [Great] Plains under a cloud-free sky and get a sunburn. Interpreting the weather incorrectly wastes both time and money."[5]

Sometimes, though, scientists get the forecast just right. They arrive at a location and out of the clear blue sky, they see cloud towers start to bubble up as if by magic. Then a violent thunderstorm takes shape before their eyes, and before long, they're suddenly face-to-face with a roaring tornado. That's when the real work begins.

Probing the Beast

Scientists usually have only a few minutes to deploy instruments around a tornado and get the data they need before the tornado moves out of range, charges at them, or dies. Each field project is different, but researchers tend to rely on the following methods for gathering important information:

Mobile Doppler radar: Scientists use trucks to bring Doppler radar units up close to a tornado. Radar behaves like a flashlight beam; the closer it is to something, the better the resolution. The scientists try to park the Doppler trucks within a mile or two from a tornado and preferably on high ground with an unobstructed view down into flatlands. They lower weights to the ground to keep the trucks from blowing away in strong gusts. Then they shoot the radar at the tornado, scanning back and

A mobile Doppler radar unit probes a supercell thunderstorm.

forth at different heights. This makes a three-dimensional map of the funnel's structure, including a record of how fast its winds blow in different regions.

Getting a good data set is actually very hard to do. Many times scientists get the trucks set up in what looks like a perfect position, but then the storm drifts off before a tornado forms, or a tornado forms but moves in a different direction than they'd anticipated, or it moves so quickly they get a chance to scan it for only a very short period of time.

Weather balloons: Weather balloons carry an instrument package high up into the atmosphere to get information about a supercell thunderstorm. The package usually includes sensors for measuring temperature, air pressure, and humidity. Researchers often release weather balloons at a variety of points during a storm to record any changes that might be occurring. Once it's released, the helium-filled balloon rises steadily and the instruments transmit data to the scientists' computers. At a certain prescribed height, the balloon bursts and its instruments parachute back to the ground where the scientists can recover them for future use.

Trial and error have taught scientists to be careful where they release a weather balloon. Howard Bluestein recalled releasing one near Gruver, Texas. "It rose promptly to the utility lines overhead and became entangled, the instrument package and its bright red balloon dangling in the wind. . . . But not all was lost. A couple of cowboys appeared, as if on cue, and lassoed the package—probably the first and only time a [weather balloon] has ever been captured Wild West style."[6]

Launching a weather balloon

Mobile mesonet

Mobile mesonet: This is a term for a fleet of cars with high-tech weather instruments mounted to their roofs. The cars zip into choreographed positions to make a "net" around a storm, and the rooftop instruments take measurements of the winds, temperature, pressure, location, and humidity. Passengers in the cars use laptop computers to digitally record voice descriptions of the storm for later reference.

Airplanes: Sometimes researchers take to the air in specially strengthened airplanes with shatterproof windshields to protect them from battering hailstones. They fly in racetrack patterns around a tornado thunderstorm and use radar devices, surveillance cameras, and other instruments to record data from the storm's core.

The Research Aviation Facility (RAF) of the National Center for Atmospheric Research (NCAR) currently uses Hercules, an EC-130Q aircraft, for research in atmospheric chemistry, cloud physics, and more.

HIAPER is a brand-new aircraft being modified for the National Science Foundation's environmental research program. HIAPER means High-performance Instrumental Airborne Platform for Environmental Research. It is scheduled for its first project in 2005 and is intended to be used for the next several decades.

Video and still-picture photography: Researchers take video footage and snap photographs of tornadoes so that later, in the quiet of their lab, they can study what happened out in the field, including the way the clouds looked before the tornado formed, the shape the tornado took, the path it followed, and the way it dispersed debris.

Turtles: These are turtle-shell-shaped canisters weighted with lead (so they won't flip over in high winds) and packed with

Turtles are designed to protect instruments from the ravages of powerful storms.

temperature and pressure gauges. Scientists attempt to lay Turtles in the path of an approaching tornado. With luck, the tornado heads in the direction they expected and passes right over the Turtles. With a little more luck, the Turtles survive to record what happened inside the funnel.

+   +   +

Researchers link their storm-chase vehicles to a satellite navigation system called the Global Positioning System (GPS). This allows them to track each vehicle's progress so that later they can figure out where they were when they recorded specific measurements. They also download GPS maps onto their laptop computers, which display where their vehicle is relative to all the highways and side roads. This can be life-saving information if a tornado suddenly veers toward the scientists and they've got to figure out how to outrun it. After all, if a tornado were chasing you, you wouldn't want to find yourself on a dead-end street!

The Core Punch

While researchers try to do everything they can to stay safe, sometimes the desire for the perfect data set leads them to take risks. Most have "core punched" storms, which means intentionally driving through the precipitation core (the wet and wild midsection of the storm) where visibility can be near zero. Here, their vehicles encounter gale-force winds, deluging rain, and baseball-sized hail. The goal is to break through to the rain-free side of the storm where the mesocyclone and updrafts occur. The biggest danger is that they might break through the storm a little too late and a tornado will have formed right in front of them.

In fierce storms, dangerous hailstones can be bigger than golf balls.

Sometimes the rain will be so strong, their windshield wipers can't keep up and they don't know they're face-to-face with a funnel. For this reason, researchers turn on the radar during a core punch and rely on it to tell them if there's a twister up ahead.

Researcher Herb Stein recalled driving a core punch in his Doppler radar truck: "The closer we got to the center of the rotation where the tornado could form, the stronger the winds and the more blinding the rain became. Leaves and small branches were being ripped from the trees and flew sideways."[7] Stein's partner kept an eye on the radar screen and suddenly shouted that a small tornado was forming just 1 mile (1.6 kilometers) straight ahead of them and directly in their path.

"Suddenly wind and debris picked up force," Stein said. "We heard a loud 'thud' as something airborne hit the side of our truck. Branches and small articles were moving horizontally across the road and the heavy rain—also moving horizontally—whited out our view of anything outside the truck. We stopped and I could feel the truck being blown forward by the powerful winds. The rain was so intense it interfered with the radar signals. . . . My mouth went completely dry as I contemplated my arrogance in wanting to keep driving into the teeth of the tornado."[8]

Luckily the researchers survived. To date no researcher has ever been killed by a tornado, but such moments can be reminders that they're dealing with powerful forces beyond their control. One tornado scientist said, "People like us love to see Mother Nature's fury. People think we're crazy and nuts. But we *love* these things."[9]

CHAPTER THREE

Project VORTEX

One scientist who loves tornadoes is NSSL researcher Erik Rasmussen. A self-described tornado nut, he first displayed a genius for forecasting when he was in college. In fact, he got so good at predicting where tornadoes would hit that older meteorologists (weather scientists) gave him the nickname "the Dryline Kid," after the drylines that separate hot and cold air masses that can sometimes lead to tornadoes.

During the springs of 1994 and 1995 the Dryline Kid led the biggest tornado experiment ever conducted. Project VORTEX

Tornado scientists of Project VORTEX (left to right): Bob Davies-Jones, Jerry Straka, and Erik Rasmussen

(Verification of the Origins of Rotation in Tornadoes Experiment) involved twenty of the top researchers in the field and one hundred university students. The plan was for everyone to swarm around one tornado at a time and gather as much data as possible on the tornado's entire life cycle, from birth to death. No other field project in history had involved so many people working simultaneously to probe every region of a tornadic storm from the ground upward into the sky. They used a fleet of mobile mesonet vehicles, four ballooning vehicles, two photography vehicles, a Doppler radar truck (which they called Doppler on Wheels or DOW), Turtles, and two aircraft. The Dryline Kid hoped VORTEX would find an answer to the big question: What causes tornadoes to form?

The Doppler radar-equipped airplanes that were part of Project VORTEX research

Preparing to Head Out

Not surprisingly, VORTEX took a lot of planning. As the field coordinator (FC), Rasmussen said it was his job "to try to bring all these instruments to the right place at the right time. I have to try to mentally project where a storm is going and what it is going to do. . . . I have to try to make sure I'm not getting anyone into a situation where the tornado's going to overtake them and they can't escape from it."[1]

He knew that some of the university students were not experienced tornado chasers, so he wanted to prepare them for what they might encounter in the field. He wrote up detailed safety instructions warning them of all sorts of possible hazards. For example, he cautioned, "Be very careful when opening your car door . . . the wind can rip the door from your grasp and spring the hinges, damaging the vehicle and potentially injuring someone standing nearby."[2] If lightning strikes while you're outside the vehicle, Rasmussen advised, squat on the balls of your feet because the bolts are attracted to the tallest objects around, and do not touch any metal fences or barbed wire.

Most of the students would be driving mobile mesonet cars (nicknamed "Probes"), and Rasmussen would stay in constant radio contact with them. He'd track their movement on his computer and arrange them into various positions around a storm. Once they were in place, their job was to drive with the storm, allowing their rooftop weather sensors to document it over several hours.

The most dangerous jobs were left to veteran tornado researchers. For example, a couple of intrepid scientists volun-

The mobile mesonets for Project VORTEX were equipped with weather sensors to document storms.

teered to lay the Turtles (which Rasmussen and colleagues had invented for VORTEX) in the projected path of the oncoming tornado. Two other scientists would drive Probe 1 directly underneath the "bear cage" or mesocyclone part of the storm for as long as possible before a tornado formed. Once it looked like a twister was about to form, Probe 1 was to maneuver to a safe position and then follow behind the tornado as closely as possible.

Foiled again?

By the start of the 1994 tornado season, every member of Project VORTEX was trained and ready to go. But Mother Nature refused to cooperate. That year there were few big tornadoes, and while the storm chasers caught some, they missed the best ones. The 1995 season wasn't shaping up to be much better. It looked like the grand experiment might turn out to be something of a disappointment. "Basically the frustration has to do with the atmosphere not behaving the way my simple little mind predicts it will behave," grumbled a discouraged Rasmussen.[3]

Some students in the project were trained to launch weather balloons while others were instructed to videotape the events.

In 1994, a Project VORTEX participant films a supercell storm that didn't produce a tornado.

On June 2, 1995, VORTEX was thirteen days away from officially ending. The Dryline Kid got up early to study the weather maps and plan where his fleet would go that day. He noticed something interesting happening near Lubbock, Texas. This was an area he knew well because he'd gone to college there. "I looked at the forecast for the Lubbock winds," he recalled, "and they were forecast to be out of the southeast at 30 mph [48 kmh] and unstable. I thought, wow, when I lived there that always meant big stuff. . . . I thought, it looks like we'll have a really typical west Texas tornado outbreak."[4]

At 10 A.M. the sun shone down on the caravan of VORTEX vehicles leaving the NSSL. When they got to Clovis, Texas, big puffy white clouds were starting to build in the sky. Everyone got out of their vehicles to wait. Time passed slowly. People put on their sunglasses and lounged on car hoods. They counted rattlesnakes on the roadside. The clouds drifted like cotton.

Steve Gaddy, a graduate student at the University of Oklahoma, was driving one of the vehicles. He wrote an e-mail to his buddies describing what was happening: "We appear to have time to wait, so we test the radar. 'In bound rock please.' We throw rocks back and forth checking the inbound and outbound velocities' detection on radar, naturally trying to hit each other as we throw them."[5]

The clouds started to darken and grow more threatening. Rasmussen shouted for everyone to get in their vehicles; they were going to follow the storm northeastward. As they drove, winds kicked up dust so thick they couldn't see the cars in front of them. Power lines crashed along the roadside. The lead vehicle radioed that rotation could now be seen in the clouds.

"When that happens," Rasmussen said, "I kick into 'robot' mode—calling people, finding out where they are and what they're seeing, triangulating on the map. . . . Once that happens, there's really no time to get excited or enjoy the storm; I'm just pretty much all business."[6]

Following the storm, the team headed 30 miles (48 kilometers) northeast toward the small Texas panhandle town of Friona. There, amid gale-force winds, a tornado formed. Rasmussen coordinated the team into position around it. The sky went black and thunder rumbled as they scanned the tornado with radar, dropped Turtles, and launched balloons. The tornado tore up a grain elevator and picked up a railroad boxcar and sent it bouncing through a cemetery before fading away in curtains of torrential rain. Rasmussen knew he hadn't gotten enough information. Then a call came through from the NSSL weather station that mesocyclones were developing just southeast of Friona. Most were projected to move across a wildlife refuge area with very few roads. Rasmussen decided, instead, to target another promising mesocyclone that was developing southwest of them near Dimmitt, Texas.

Steve Gaddy recalled that as they left Friona they encountered "two semi [trucks] turned on their sides blocking that road. . . . We just crossed the railroad track, which had gates going crazy as a 76-car train was derailed in the area with cars thrown off the track, when we literally ran into a power line stretched across the road. . . . We felt lucky to be able to just back up, without harm."[7]

Once the VORTEX team safely reached the Dimmitt area, they began gathering data as a big mesocyclone bore down on them. Buffeting winds sent the vehicles rocking, and hail dented their hoods. Their windshield wipers were useless. "It was really scary," said Josh Wurman, the DOW driver. "We couldn't see the tornado and didn't know if, at any second, it would suddenly appear and mow us down."[8]

Blinded by torrents of rain, Wurman suddenly plunged the Doppler truck off the road and into a drainage ditch. Jumping out into the storm, he ran behind the truck and started pushing. A colleague gunned the engine and the tires spun. Wurman got hit by mud and cow manure, but he kept pushing until they got the truck free and back on the road. Parking near a cemetery outside Dimmitt, Wurman trained the radar on the increasingly ferocious storm.

The cloud base was lowering to the ground and showing rapid rotation. The driver of Probe 1 anxiously radioed Ras-

The cloud base over Dimmitt looks fierce.

mussen: "There's rapid motion just to our SW; dust on the ground; I don't know what it's connected to."[9]

Rasmussen radioed back that he saw a large funnel near them. A moment later he said, "Probe 1, [this is] FC, we see a tornado."[10]

Steve Gaddy recalled his awe at the "huge tornado roaring about 12 miles [19 kilometers] to our west just south of Dimmitt.

The Dimmitt tornado has formed in the distance.

It was an awesome sight! We instantly knew it was a maxi-tornado with very, very damaging potential."[11] As it raced along, the tornado snapped power poles and tore up hundreds of feet of asphalt, spraying it into surrounding fields.

Overhead, Howard Bluestein was capturing data from an airplane. "Flying at only a thousand feet [305 meters] above the ground, we were tossed about mercilessly by turbulence," he recalled. "We probed the storms blindly, unable to see the tornado or to get closer."[12] He'd never gotten airsick on a mission before, but "the plane was yawing—it had a lot of side-to-side motion. We were flying in the boundary layer and really getting bounced around. . . . I should have had something to eat [before takeoff], but there were large tornadoes going on outside and . . . there was no time to sit and have a leisurely meal, no time to eat anything."[13]

On the ground, Rasmussen was trying to radio the Probe drivers and get a fix on everyone's positions, but no one would respond. "What happened at Dimmitt was that the tornado formed and everybody was just mesmerized," he said. "I mean it was a beautiful sight. And for about 40 seconds, I couldn't get anybody to tell me . . . [how far] the tornado was from their vehicle. . . . No one would tell me anything."[14]

Rasmussen didn't know if people were doing their jobs or not. He admitted he got "incredibly frustrated and started punching my fists into the roof [of the van] and pounding on the table and swearing and cussing. . . . In my whole life I've never been high-strung or angry or violent. I'm just kind of a laid-back person. . . . But I had . . . people out there and all this time and money invested."[15]

The tornado travels close to the Probes.

Success at Last

The next morning, Rasmussen made the announcement: VOR-TEX had obtained the largest data set ever from a tornado. Videotape captured the tornado from several angles and as close as 3 miles (4.8 kilometers) away. The Probes collected one thousand automated weather observations from around the storm, and more data were gathered by a number of weather balloons. The airplane team had recorded continuous radar on winds spinning in the updraft. The Doppler truck received stunning radar detail of the tornado's interior structure, including the hollow core, debris cloud, and 3-D imagery of where the maximum winds had been located. Rasmussen was thrilled. "I think we'll eventually be rewriting some books on tornadoes," he said.[16]

Today, researchers are still poring over the data gathered at Dimmitt and realizing that tornadoes are even more complicated than they previously thought. "We sort of cast a wide net to see what we could catch," said Rasmussen, "and it turned out that it seems like everything that's important for tornado formation goes on in some tiny area about 2 miles [3.2 kilometers] across in the back side of the storm. Had we known that at the time, we would have concentrated all of our vehicles and all of our observations in that area, but we didn't know it."[17]

Most research projects in the years since VORTEX have focused smaller teams on this rear region of the storm. In 2001, Rasmussen and his colleagues launched another big storm chase and they made what he said was a "staggering" discovery: The storms that produce tornadoes tend to have warm, humid RFD air plunging to the ground, while storms that don't produce tornadoes tend to have cool and dry air in this region. "We're very interested in the quality of that air," said one researcher.[18]

This image is considered to be one of the earliest photographs ever taken of a tornado. It was captured by photographer A. A. Adams on April 23, 1884, in Anderson County, Kansas.

CHAPTER FOUR

Unlocking the Whirlwind's Mysteries

America's first tornado scientist was John Park Finley. A tall bear of a man, Finley grew up on a prosperous Michigan farm where he learned to keep a close eye on the weather because of its powerful effect on crops. In 1877, Finley enlisted with the U.S. Army Signal Service (later called the Signal Corps), where he received meteorological training and developed a keen interest in tornadoes. A couple of years later, the army sent Finley to study damage caused by a rash of twisters that had swept through the Midwest. Traveling cross-country by horse and buggy, he toured the devastated regions, interviewing eyewitnesses and making meticulous maps showing the twisters' paths. Struck by what he'd witnessed, Finley embarked on an exhaustive study of other tornadoes.

In 1882 he suggested the War Department study an entire tornado season by posting a weather observer in Kansas City, Missouri, who could telegraph reports of severe storms heading across the plains from the East to the West. The plan was approved and Finley served as head of the program. He recruited storm spotters from all over the region to relay weather information straight to his office. With this limited data, Finley began issuing tornado warnings. In 1884 he correctly predicted twenty-eight of one hundred tornadoes. These results weren't good enough for the U.S. government, however. Fearing that false alarms caused people to unnecessarily panic, they banned Finley and all meteorologists from using the word *tornado* in their forecasts. With this ruling, tornado research in the United States ground to a halt until the 1940s.

Luck Was on Their Side

On the morning of March 20, 1948, at Oklahoma City's Tinker Air Base, two air force meteorologists—Captain Robert Miller and his boss Major Ernest J. Fawbush—issued a forecast for gusty winds and possible thunderstorms. Instead, a tornado roared through the base. It rolled big aircraft like they were toys, causing ten million dollars worth of damage and injuring several men in the control tower. The base commander was furious. Couldn't Fawbush and Miller have predicted the tornado? That afternoon the meteorologists started poring through weather charts, analyzing the conditions that existed before every recorded tornado. They noted similarities in the weather patterns.

On March 25, Fawbush and Miller woke up to find these same telltale weather patterns threatening their area. Throughout the morning, conditions deteriorated. The meteorologists debated what to do. Miller estimated that the odds that another tornado would strike the base in a single week were about 20 million to 1. He had visions of what would happen if he told his commander to prepare for a twister and he was wrong again. "I wondered how I would manage as a civilian, perhaps as an elevator operator. It seemed improbable that anyone would employ, as a weather forecaster, an idiot who issued a tornado forecast for a precise location."[1]

But finally he and Fawbush decided they couldn't live with themselves if another tornado hit and people got hurt. At 2:50 P.M. they issued a tornado watch. Aircraft were lashed down and stored in hangars. Personnel fled dangerous areas like the control tower. At 3:00 P.M. thunderstorms began to form, and at 6:00 P.M. a tornado hit the base.

The Fawbush–Miller tornado forecast was one of the luckiest in history. Even today meteorologists can't say three hours ahead of time that a tornado will strike a particular place on the map. "We're still amazed that they could issue a forecast and have it hit when it did," said meteorologist Steven Weiss.[2]

Lucky or not, Fawbush and Miller had identified the basic weather patterns that lead to tornadoes. After that, the air force began to predict twisters using their technique. Sometimes the predictions were right, but sometimes tornadoes formed in areas where they hadn't been expected. It was clear that the Fawbush–Miller method had value but needed to be refined.

The airplanes on Tinker Air Force Base were tossed around and destroyed by the tornado that swept through Oklahoma City on March 25, 1948. The air force began to make tornado predictions after this incident.

The air force forecasts were supposed to be kept private, but a few of them leaked out. A 1951 article in the *Saturday Evening Post* said, "A high percentage of [the air force] tornado predictions has been verified. This year, in March and April, the Fawbush-Miller-severe-storm-forecasting technique correctly called the turn on seven twisters—four in Oklahoma, one in Arkansas, and two in Texas."[3] The public began to clamor for access to this information. In 1952 the U.S. Weather Service agreed to start broadcasting tornado warnings.

What's on My Radar Screen?

A year later, a tornado passed near Champaign, Illinois, and a radar operator noticed a strange hook shape on his screen. It did not look like anything he'd ever seen before and seemed to be related to the thunderstorm outside. Later analysis showed that the hook had followed the tornado's exact path. Had he accidentally captured the first-ever radar image of a tornado?

A brilliant young tornado researcher named Tetsuya Theodore Fujita came to Urbana, Illinois, to try to figure it out. There were only limited data from the storm and yet he kept delving deeper and deeper into the numbers, doing calculations, and relying on geometry to push his theories forward. He showed that there was actually a wealth of material hidden in the data. "Reading the analysis Fujita made of the Champaign radar findings," said one meteorologist, "is like opening one of those hollow wooden Russian dolls, only to find a dozen more layers of dolls inside."[4]

With a virtuoso's flourish, Ted Fujita drew complicated maps of the tornado and its storm. He proved that the hook was not the tornado itself, but belonged to a rotation up in the thunderclouds. He said this rotation resembled "a miniature hurricane in many respects."[5] He named the mini-hurricane the "mesocyclone." Fujita's discovery of the mesocyclone's radar signature meant that forecasters had a valuable new tool for identifying potential tornadic storms. Soon, the government decided to install radar towers across Tornado Alley to watch for Fujita's mesocyclones.

Mr. Tornado

One writer said, "Ted Fujita somehow consistently found the clues others overlooked. He was probably the best meteorological detective who ever lived."[6] Fujita proved his sleuthing talents in 1957 after a tornado raced through Fargo, North Dakota. He asked a local radio announcer to urge listeners to mail in any photos or movies they'd taken of the twister. Soon, Fujita's desk was buried under material. Obsessively precise, Fujita spent years poring over the photos and movie stills, determining exactly where they'd been shot, at what time, and at what distance from the storm. Bit by bit he pieced together a breathtakingly detailed history of the storm.

This endeavor hooked Fujita on photography. In 1965 a tornado outbreak hit six Midwestern states. Fujita rented a Cessna airplane and, for four days, flew repeatedly over the paths of the tornadoes taking photos of the damage. Studying the shots back in his lab, he noticed overlapping swirls in a cornfield. His colleagues thought a plow must have done it, but Fujita wasn't so sure. Using a magnifier, he realized that the loops were actually debris. What forces could account for these patterns?

Finally Fujita figured it out: Tornadoes were not always simple whirling funnels. Rather, some contained smaller intense funnels that he called "suction vortices." These suction vortices spun around the larger central funnel and sucked things up, leaving behind the peculiar looping patterns. Fujita's discovery meant that tornadoes were much more structurally complex than previously assumed. Suction vortices also helped explain some legendary tales of tornado mischief. For example, there's the story

Ted Fujita works with an early machine that simulated tornadoes in the 1970s.

one tornado survivor told of a wall clock downstairs that, "went upstairs, made a right-angle turn in our bedroom, [and] was lying on the bed. The roof was gone, the bedspread was still on the bed and my shoes were under the bed yet, not disturbed."[7]

How could this be possible? According to Fujita's theory, the suction vortices act like vacuum cleaners except that they don't always pick up everything in their path. Some items may remain untouched while others get lifted into the storm and spit out somewhere else. Even if a house is right in a tornado's path, the winds won't be blowing at the same speed everywhere, and the smaller suction vortices may hit one room and not another. They can pick up a clock and deposit it upstairs but not even touch a nearby pair of shoes.

Fujita Scale

Fujita's photos of tornado damage also led him to conclude that tornadoes don't maintain their strength the whole time, but rather get stronger and weaker at different points along the way. To illustrate this, he started working on a way to rate a tornado's intensity at different points. While it might seem like a tornado's size would tell you how strong it is, this isn't true. A few monster tornadoes that are a mile or more wide can churn across the countryside for an hour or more, and while they may look more impressive, a thin ropelike twister can be just as destructive.

Fujita determined that the best way to classify tornadoes is by the damage they cause. He organized a scale on which the weakest tornado (one that breaks off tree branches and topples small saplings) would be listed as an F0 tornado. The strongest tornado would be an F5, capable of damaging steel-reinforced buildings and throwing cars hundreds of feet through the air. While the Fujita scale is useful, it also has problems. Many tornadoes occur in open country where there's nothing to damage. Also, it's impossible to say for certain how sturdy a building was before it got hit. "Every home is nailed together differently, anchored differently, built of different materials," explained meteorologist Tom Grazulis.[8]

Tetsuya Theodore Fujita developed his famous F-scale without ever having seen an actual tornado. Every time he tried to

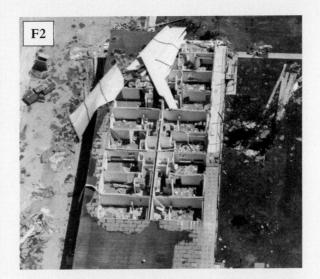

FUJITA SCALE

Scale	Wind Speed MPH (km)	Expected Damage
F0	40–72 (64–116)	Light Damage
F1	73–112 (117–181)	Moderate Damage
F2	113–157 (182–253)	Considerable Damage
F3	158–206 (254–331)	Severe Damage
F4	207–260 (332–419)	Devastating Damage
F5	261–318 (420–512)	Incredible Damage

find one, he struck out. His license plate read "TTF000" as a joke about his tornado observation record. Finally in 1982, Fujita witnessed his first tornado. One friend recalled that Fujita was so excited, "for days, he was taking people out to dinner."[9]

Doppler Radar

While Fujita was studying the aftermath of tornadoes, other researchers were working on a new type of radar technology—Doppler radar—that would allow them to probe the live beasts.

Doppler radar relies on something called the Doppler effect, named after Christian Doppler, an Austrian physicist who explained the phenomenon. This effect is probably already familiar to you from hearing ambulance sirens. When a siren is coming toward you, it sounds higher in pitch; when it is going away from you, the siren's pitch lowers. The Doppler effect accounts for this pitch change of inbound/outbound motion.

In the early 1970s, scientists at the newly formed NSSL tried bouncing Doppler radar beams off water droplets in clouds and found that there was a change in pitch depending on whether those droplets moved toward the radar or away from it. Conventional radar could show only the intensity of hail or rain in a storm, but not how that precipitation might be rotating. Doppler radar allowed scientists to watch a mesocyclone pick up speed as it turned in tighter and tighter swirls. Could they identify a developing tornado by certain swirling patterns? To find out, someone had to leave the lab and report back about what was going on in real life. In 1972 the Tornado Intercept Project was born.

Storm Chasing

Howard Bluestein recalled joining the Tornado Intercept Project in 1977: "There were two cars and I decided, gee, this looks interesting. I think I'd like to try this. . . . Not many people considered [storm chasing] scientific back then. They thought we were just going out to have thrills and spills."[10]

If the scientists in the lab saw something interesting on the Doppler radar, they'd radio, or what they called "nowcast," Bluestein and tell him where to go to investigate. Bluestein and a partner would drive as fast as they could to that area and then report back, "We see a tornado now," or "No tornado but we've got a certain type of wind." They would then film the storms to document them.

Bluestein recalled the day he chased down his first tornado:

By late afternoon we were on the track of a [potentially] tornadic storm. . . . According to the nowcaster, the tornado [might be] heading for Tipton, in southwestern Oklahoma. . . . We turned west on a narrow paved road. It was hazy, and visibility was only a few miles. Suddenly, just to the southwest, the silhouette of a huge cylinder appeared crossing the road ahead of us. . . . Excitement—and inexperience—got the best of us. The member of our crew assigned to shoot 16-millimeter movies of the tornadoes we happened upon panicked and froze, unable to do anything. . . . I soon ran out of film, and in my haste I began to unload the exposed film before rewinding it. Fortunately, only several frames were lost as a result. . . . [11]

Dawn of the Computer Age

By the 1980s tornado scientists were turning to mathematicians to get help simulating tornadoes on powerful computers. They figured that if they could slowly pick apart a simulated storm in the safety of their laboratory, they might learn much about the forces at work inside real storms.

In order to design accurate computer models, the mathematicians needed to plug in real numbers taken from real storms. Among other things, the mathematicians wanted to know exactly how far the pressure dropped inside each funnel and how fast the winds had been blowing. Somehow, tornado scientists had to come up with a way to get data from *inside* the tornado. "The main challenge," stated Bluestein, "apart from ensuring our own safety, was to design an instrument that could withstand the force of a tornado."[12]

TOTO

In 1980, Bluestein hit the road with a squat 400-pound (181-kilogram) cylinder strapped to the flatbed of his pickup truck. The instrument was named TOTO (totable tornado observatory) after the dog who, along with his owner, Dorothy, was blown away by a tornado in *The Wizard of Oz*. The mechanical TOTO was constructed by Al Bedard and Carl Ramzy of the National Oceanic and Atmospheric Administration (NOAA) in collaboration with Howard Bluestein.

"In theory," said Bluestein, "we would get in the direct path of a tornado, roll TOTO down the truck's ramp, switch on the instrument package, and get . . . out of the way. . . . The tornado would, we reasoned, pass over TOTO, probably leaving it somewhat battered but (we hoped) still intact. We would then retrieve our mechanical canine and interpret the data traces."[13]

TOTO was the model for a device called Dorothy in the 1996 movie *Twister.* In that movie, Dorothy is loaded with sensors that are released when the scientists finally manage to stick her in the path of a tornado.

In real life, Bluestein didn't have such luck. "The problem was, every time we got in the path of a tornado, the tornado would either change direction or disappear," he said.[14] Even as Bluestein grew increasingly frustrated with the unwieldy TOTO, the media were falling in love with it. "Press and media accounts of what we were trying to do had captured, apparently, the imagination of the public," he said. "One day out in rural

TOTO was built to withstand gusting winds over 100 miles (160 kilometers) per hour and had devices to measure wind velocity, pressure, and temperature inside a funnel.

north-central Oklahoma, just ahead of a storm, we set up TOTO on the front yard of a rural house. The owners must have recognized us and, guessing what we were doing, ran . . . for cover. Of course. . . no tornado formed. . . . Perhaps the reaction of people seeing us arrive on their front lawn with TOTO should have been one of relief."[15]

By 1985, Bluestein decided to retire TOTO. That same year he got a call from an engineer who told him that scientists at the Los Alamos National Laboratory had designed a portable Doppler unit. Would it help to bring radar up close to a tornado? "Indeed it would," Bluestein asserted.[16]

This ushered in a decade of technological innovation. Researchers built the first DOW truck and designed the easy-to-maneuver Turtles. They perfected the instrument packages attached to weather balloons and developed the concept of the mobile mesonet. Eventually, all of these advancements culminated in that grand experiment, Project VORTEX.

Today, after half a century of experimentation and research, twisters remain one of nature's greatest unsolved mysteries. "For every question we answer about severe storms and tornadoes, we probably raise 10 to 100 more," said scientist Gilbert Sebenste. "In summing up tornado research in the last 100 years, it can best be summarized as, 'the more we know, the more we realize we don't know.' . . . We knew we had a long road ahead, and it's perhaps an even longer road than we thought."[17]

Looking to the Future

With a few clicks of his mouse, meteorology professor Bruce Lee can bring up a very realistic-looking computer image of four ropy tornadoes spiraling beneath a large billowing thunderstorm. He created these tornadoes by plugging in data that storm chasers gathered from a family of four real tornadoes, almost identical to the ones on his screen. "When we show tornado researchers the animation from these model results, they are just astounded by how well this matches what they've seen," said Lee.[18]

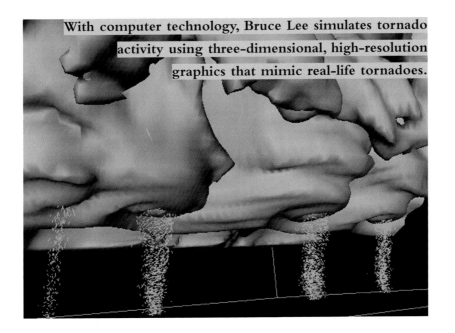

With computer technology, Bruce Lee simulates tornado activity using three-dimensional, high-resolution graphics that mimic real-life tornadoes.

Using new superfast computers, scientists are starting to experiment on simulated tornadoes in ways they couldn't possibly do with real ones. For example, they are studying what happens when environmental conditions change around a tornado. What if the wind is coming from a different direction? What if there's no lightning? What if the ground is a few degrees hotter? Bit by bit, scientists are using simulated tornadoes to isolate the critical factors that must be present if a storm is going to spawn a tornado.

Cutting-Edge Developments

Out in the real world, scientists want to zero in on the intriguing RFDs. The challenge is to safely gather comprehensive data from this violent region of a storm. Researchers at NSSL, in collaboration with the aerospace engineering department at the University of Colorado, recently built a small remote-controlled instrumented aircraft (with a wingspan of about 6.5 feet [2 meters]) designed to fly through RFDs and take measurements. This aircraft will hopefully reap vital data without risking human life. Other scientists are developing a new generation of cutting-edge Turtles to survey the quality of RFD air at ground level. They plan to deploy these Turtles in a VORTEX-style experiment tentatively scheduled to occur sometime between 2005 and 2008.

Advancements in radar technology also hold great promise. Traditional radar transmits radio pulses in a horizontal direction, while new "dual-polarization" radar includes vertical orientation as well. This allows scientists to determine not only the movement of a storm, but also the size and shape of its precipitation (such as ice, rain, and hail). By training these dual-polarization radar devices on RFDs, researchers hope to determine which types of precipitation are linked to tornadoes. Erik Rasmussen said, "Incorporating . . . general storm environment data with [these sorts of new] Doppler radar signatures holds hope of greatly improved warnings."[19]

Build a Better House

The best tornado forecast won't save lives if people don't have somewhere secure to take shelter. That's why the government pours research dollars into projects that explore ways to construct buildings to better withstand severe weather. At Texas Tech University, an indoor wind laboratory re-creates the various types of gusts associated with tornadic storms. "It is a bit hard to just wait on nature to give us strong winds to look at wind flow around buildings, wind pressures, and wind forces on buildings," said one professor. "We use the wind tunnel to simulate nature and speed up the research."[20]

One afternoon wind-lab students gathered around giant cannons that they loaded with two-by-fours, metal pipes, and chunks

Texas Tech's tornado simulator produces a tornado-like vortex over a model building that contains devices to measure its pressure. As the tornado passes over the model, the data are recorded and later analyzed.

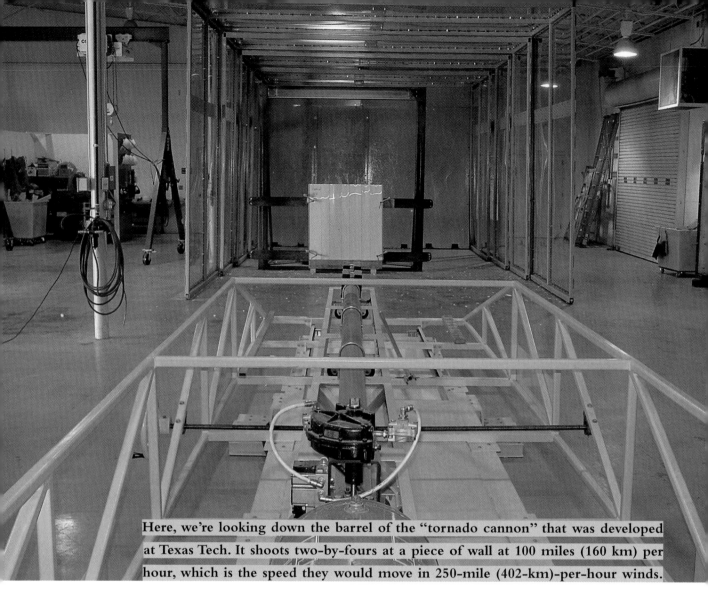

Here, we're looking down the barrel of the "tornado cannon" that was developed at Texas Tech. It shoots two-by-fours at a piece of wall at 100 miles (160 km) per hour, which is the speed they would move in 250-mile (402-km)-per-hour winds.

of hail. They fired this "tornadic debris" into various wall materials to see which one held up best. Experiments like these are used by engineers to construct "safe rooms," which people can add to their homes, that offer protection from winds up to 250 miles (402 kilometers) per hour.

CHAPTER FIVE

Become a Tornado Scientist!

Most tornado scientists got their start by watching the skies when they were young. In the second grade, meteorologist Tom Moore did a weather report for his class newspaper. After that he was hooked: "I was head over heels involved with weather," he admitted.[1] He especially loved big snowstorms, when he'd watch the first flakes start to fall just as his local weather forecasters had predicated. Other tornado scientists report that they became excited about severe

Tornado scientists put themselves in considerable danger to gather critical data that could save many lives.

weather from images they saw on television or stories they read in books and magazines.

If you decide you want to become a tornado researcher, you'll need a strong background in math, physics, chemistry, and computer science. In high school, take as many of these classes as you can. You may also want to join the Skywarn network in your area. Skywarn is made up of amateur storm spotters who are trained to observe severe weather in their own areas and pass critical information on to the National Weather Service (NWS). The NWS offers spotter training sessions in various locations nationwide.

There are many colleges that offer degree programs in atmospheric sciences and meteorology. If you go to a college in Tornado Alley, you may have an opportunity to participate in tornado field research. With a bachelor of science degree you can become a weather forecaster and start working with organizations like the NWS or NSSL. If you want to lead a tornado research project, you will need a Ph.D. Erik Rasmussen said, "A young person interested in being a tornado scientist will have to be on the academically rigorous track . . . as early as their high school years. . . . [Tornado science is] a small field, and we need only encourage the few who really have a passion for it."[2]

Mike Foster, a meteorologist with the NWS, claimed that he started studying tornadoes and chasing storms because "I love big skies and flat land and small towns. On days when [tornadic] opportunity is high and storms are all around, there's an almost romantic spirit about driving around out here over these plains, observing the . . . power of nature. . . . Most people go through their lives paying very little attention to the sky."[3]

When a Tornado Strikes

There's a difference between a tornado *watch* and a tornado *warning*. A watch means that severe weather might occur over the next several hours. Tornado watches usually cover a large area of about 140 miles by 200 miles (225 kilometers by 322 kilometers) and do not mean that a tornado will form, rather that you should stay alert to the possibility. You can stay up-to-date on developments by listening to the radio or watching TV.

Tornado *warnings* are issued for much smaller areas once a tornado has actually been spotted on the ground nearby or the Doppler radar indicates that a mesocyclone that can spawn a tornado is present. As soon as a warning is issued, you should seek shelter. The best place to wait out a tornado is in a specially designed "safe room" or in a basement. If neither is available, go to an inner closet or bathroom on the ground floor. People used to think it was a good idea to open windows, but that's not true. Opening windows actually allows damaging winds to whip through your house and wastes valuable time.

If you are outside, lie flat in a low-lying spot or ditch and cover your head with your arms. Mobile homes fare very badly in tornadoes and should be left immediately. Occasionally tornadoes form so quickly that no warning is possible. For this reason, seek shelter if the sky darkens and develops a greenish hue. You should also seek shelter if large hail starts to fall, or if you hear a roar similar to that of a freight train.

Glossary of Terms

Doppler radar: Calculates both the speed and movement of an object traveling to or away from its antennae.

DOW: DOW stands for Doppler on Wheels. These are portable Doppler radar units secured to the backs of flatbed trucks and operated in the field by intercept teams. They can obtain high-resolution images of many tornado features, including wind speeds.

F-scale: Developed by Ted Fujita, it is a way to rank a tornado's intensity.

mesocyclone: The rotating section of a supercell thunderstorm that tornadoes sometimes develop below.

mobile mesonet: A fleet of specially equipped vehicles that surrounds a tornadic storm in order to take various weather-based measurements.

radar: Detects the presence and location of an object by bouncing an energy beam off it and measuring the time it takes for the signal to return.

suction vortices: Small funnels that spin around a tornado's larger funnel and suck up things similar to vacuum cleaners. The highest winds in a tornado are usually concentrated here.

supercell: A highly energetic thunderstorm that has the potential to spawn tornadoes.

tornado: A violently rotating column of air stretching between a thunderstorm and the ground.

Tornado Alley: A nickname for a section of the Midwest where there's a high occurrence of tornadoes, which roughly encompasses the states lying between the Mississippi River and the high plains—Texas, Oklahoma, Kansas, Nebraska, Iowa, Missouri, Arkansas, and Louisiana.

wall cloud: Looks like a boat rudder when it lowers from a mesocyclone. It often precedes a tornado.

waterspout: Weak tornado that forms over water.

wind shear: Winds that blow in different directions or speeds at different altitudes.

<h1>Source Notes</h1>

Introduction

1. Keay Davidson, *Twister: The Science of Tornadoes and the Making of an Adventure Movie* (New York: Pocket Books, 1996), p. 131.
2. Davidson, p. 131.
3. Jeff Rosenfeld, "Spin Doctors," *Weatherwise,* April–May 1996, p. 25.

Chapter One: Tornado!

1. Susan Burton, "Prom," *This American Life,* National Public Radio, June 8, 2001.
2. Linda Wertheimer, "Tornado," *All Things Considered,* National Public Radio, April 23, 2001.
3. Wertheimer.
4. Wertheimer.
5. Burton.
6. Burton.
7. Keay Davidson, *Twister: The Science of Tornadoes and the Making of an Adventure Movie* (New York: Pocket Books, 1996), p. 18.
8. "Inside Tornadoes." [Online] Available at http://www.weather.com/newscenter/specialreports/tornado/index.html, August 21, 2002.
9. Joe Nick Patoski, "Riders on the Storm," *Texas Monthly,* July 1996, p. 72.

Chapter Two: Chasing Twisters out on the Plains

1. Howard B. Bluestein, "Riders on the Storm: Tornado Chasers Seek the Birthplace of an Elusive Monster," *The Sciences,* March–April 1995, p. 28.
2. William Hauptman, "On the Dryline: Chasing Tornadoes in the Texas Panhandle with Meteorologists from the National Severe Storms Laboratory," *The Atlantic,* May 1984, p. 78.

3. Jeff Rosenfeld, "Spin Doctors," *Weatherwise,* April–May 1996, p. 25.

4. Keay Davidson, *Twister: The Science of Tornadoes and the Making of an Adventure Movie* (New York: Pocket Books, 1996), p. 17.

5. Tim Marshall, "A Passion for Prediction," *Weatherwise,* April–May 1993, p. 23.

6. Howard B. Bluestein, *Tornado Alley: Monster Storms of the Great Plains* (New York: Oxford University Press, 1999), p. 110.

7. Herb Stein, "Storm Chasers Face the Powerful Forces of Nature." [Online] Available at http://news.nationalgeographic.com/news/2001/06/0611_stormchaser3.html, June 11, 2001.

8. Stein.

9. Davidson, p. 156.

Chapter Three: Project VORTEX

1. *Savage Skies: Riders on the Storm,* Granada/WNET video, 1996.

2. "Storm Intercept: Safety and Personal Considerations," [Online] Available at http://mrd3.nssl.ucar.edu/~vortex/OpsPlan/Ch/_Safety.html, April 25, 2002.

3. *Savage Skies: Riders on the Storm.*

4. Keay Davidson, *Twister: The Science of Tornadoes and the Making of an Adventure Movie* (New York: Pocket Books, 1996), p. 30.

5. Steve Gaddy, "Deep in the Heart of Texas." [Online] Available at http://www.usatoday.com/weather/wvor14.htm, April 25, 2002.

6. Davidson, p. 31.

7. Gaddy.

8. Devera Pine, "Chasing Twister." http://www.findarticles.com/cf_0/m1590/n12_v54/20474334/p1/article.jhtml?term=William+Hauptman+and+tornadoes, April 4, 2002.

9. "VORTEX: Unraveling the Secrets." [Online] Available at http://www.nssl.noaa.gov/noaastory/book.html, August 21, 2002.

10. "VORTEX: Unraveling the Secrets."

11. Gaddy.

12. Howard B. Bluestein, *Tornado Alley: Monster Storms of the Great Plains* (New York: Oxford University Press, 1999), p. 145.

13. Howard B. Bluestein, "Riders on the Storm: Tornado Chasers Seek the Birthplace of an Elusive Monster," *The Sciences,* March–April 1995, p. 26.

14. Davidson, p. 32.

15. Davidson, p. 11.

16. "Project Helps Scientists Understand Tornadoes." [Online] Available at http://www.usatoday.com/weather/wvor2.htm, February 8, 2000.

17. "Tracking Tornadoes." [Online] Available at http://www.weather.com/newscenter/specialreports/, May 5, 2002.

18. Chris Cappella, "Storm Troopers: On the Road with STEPS—The Largest Chase on Earth," *Weatherwise,* November–December 2000, p. 17.

Chapter Four: Unlocking the Whirlwind's Mysteries

1. "1948 Prediction Spurs Tornado Forecasting." [Online] Available at http://www.usatoday.com/weather/tornado/w1stfcst.htm, March 14, 2000.

2. "1948 Prediction Spurs Tornado Forecasting."

3. "1948 Prediction Spurs Tornado Forecasting."

4. Jeff Rosenfeld, "Mr. Tornado: The Life and Career of Ted Fujita," *Weatherwise,* May–June 1999, pp. 21–22.

5. Keay Davidson, *Twister: The Science of Tornadoes and the Making of an Adventure Movie* (New York: Pocket Books, 1996), p. 78.

6. Rosenfeld, p. 18.

7. Arjen and Jerrine Verkaik, *Under the Whirlwind: Everything You Need to Know About Tornadoes But Didn't Know Who to Ask* (Ontario: Whirlwind Books, 1997), p. 38.

8. "Dial F for Frustration: Revisiting the Fujita Scale," *Weatherwise,* June–July 1997, p. 28.

9. Rosenfeld, p. 23.

10. Jeff Rosenfeld, "Spin Doctors," *Weatherwise,* April–May 1996, p. 20.

11. Howard B. Bluestein, *Tornado Alley: Monster Storms of the Great Plains* (New York: Oxford University Press, 1999), p. 62.

12. Howard B. Bluestein, "Riders on the Storm: Tornado Chasers Seek the Birthplace of an Elusive Monster," *The Sciences,* March–April 1995, p. 29.

13. Bluestein, *Tornado Alley: Monster Storms of the Great Plains,* p. 94.

14. "Tracking Tornadoes." [Online] Available at http://www.weather.com/newscenter/specialreports/, May 5, 2002.

15. Bluestein, *Tornado Alley: Monster Storms of the Great Plains,* p. 103.

16. Bluestein, "Riders on the Storm: Tornado Chasers Seek the Birthplace of an Elusive Monster," p. 29.

17. Davidson, p. 172.

18. Daniel Pendick, "Virtual Vortex: Landspout in a Box," *Weatherwise,* May–June 1998, p. 26.

19. Erik Rasmussen, in written correspondence with author, August 20, 2002.

20. Preston Files, "Engineering Tunnel Simulates Tornado, Severe Winds." [Online] Available at http://www.universitydaily.net/vnews/display.v/ART/2002/04/29/3ccc756b2ea94, April 29, 2002.

Chapter Five: Become a Tornado Scientist!

1. "A Career Guide for the Atmospheric Sciences." [Online] Available at http://www.ametsoc.org/AMS/AtmosCareers/index.html, May 5, 2002.

2. Erik Rasmussen, in written correspondence with author, August 20, 2002.

3. Carolyn Poirot, "Storm Chasers," *Knight-Ridder/Tribune News Service,* August 11, 2000.

Further Reading

Allaby, Michael. *Dangerous Weather: A Chronology of Weather.* New York: Facts On File, 1998.

Allaby, Michael. *Dangerous Weather: Tornadoes.* New York: Facts On File, 1997.

Allaby, Michael, and Philip Eden. *Secret Worlds: Tornadoes.* New York: DK Publishing, 2001.

Berger, Melvin. *Do Tornadoes Really Twist? Questions and Answers about Tornadoes and Hurricanes.* New York: Scholastic Reference, 2000.

Boekhoff, P.M., and Stuart A. Kallen. *Tornadoes.* San Diego: Kidhaven, 2002.

Chambers, Catherine. *Disasters in Nature: Tornadoes.* Chicago: Heinemann Library, 2001.

Galiano, Dean. *Weather Watchers' Library: Tornadoes.* New York: Rosen Publishing Group, 1999.

Llewellyn, Claire. *Wild, Wet and Windy: The Weather from Tornadoes to Lightning.* Cambridge, MA: Candlewick Press, 1997.

Morris, Neil. *Wonders of Our World: Tornadoes and Hurricanes.* New York: Crabtree Publishing, 1998.

Sherrow, Victoria. *Plains Outbreak Tornadoes: Killer Twisters.* Berkeley Heights, NJ: Enslow Publishers, 1998.

Steele, Christy. *Nature on the Rampage: Tornadoes.* Austin, TX: Raintree Steck-Vaughn, 2000.

Thompson, Luke. *Natural Disasters: Tornadoes.* Danbury, CT: Children's Press, 2000.

Trueit, Trudi Strain. *Storm Chasers.* Danbury, CT: Franklin Watts, 2002.

White, Matt. *Storm Chasers: On the Trail of Deadly Tornadoes.* Mankato, MN: Capstone Press, 2002.

Web Sites

Doppler On Wheels (DOW): aaron.ou.edu/xband/

Erik Rasmussen (VORTEX leader) Home Page:
    www.nssl.noaa.gov/~erik/www/SSR/index.htm

Explore Zone Tornado Science: www.explorezone.com/weather/tornadoes.htm

(in)Famous Storm Chase Vehicles:
    www.stormeyes.org/tornado/vehicles/index.html

National Geographic: Eye in the Sky: Tornadoes:
    www.nationalgeographic.com/eye/tornadoes/science.html

National Oceanic and Atmospheric Administration Tornado Page:
    www.noaa.gov/tornadoes.html

National Severe Storms Laboratory: www.nssl.noaa.gov/

National Skywarn Page: www.skywarn.org/

NCAR/ATD Research Aviation Facility: raf.atd.ucar.edu/

Storm Prediction Center: www.spc.noaa.gov/faq/index.html

Storm Track: The Storm Chasers Home Page: www.stormtrack.org/

Tornado Project: www.tornadoproject.com/

Tornado and Storm Research Organization: www.torro.org.uk/

USA Today Tornado Information Site:
    www.usatoday.com/weather/tornado/wtwist0.htm

Vortex, Unraveling the Secrets: www.nssl.noaa.gov/noaastory/book.html

Index

Page numbers in italics
refer to illustrations.